GW01003351

The King of Puddings

ANGELA DIXON

"Far away in the distance the august mountain Kilimanjaro shone in the upper air like a vast celestial mould of Christmas pudding streaked with frozen rivers of brandy-butter."

Edward Marsh, *A number of people*, 1939

Text © Angela Dixon
Illustrations © Spider Creative

Published 2016
Spider Books

SPIDERBOOKS.CO.UK

ISBN 978-0-9561084-3-2

Printed in Gloucestershire, England on certified sustainable paper and board
Hand finished with biodegradable glitter

CONTENTS

The
Christmas
PUDDING

THE CHRISTMAS PUDDING, dark, glistening, emanating alcoholic fumes and bathed in flames, is borne in triumph as the climax of the Christmas celebrations.

It is a quintessentially English dish, yet many of its ingredients come from faraway lands. This book takes us on a world tour of the plants used as ingredients in the Christmas pudding.

The Christmas pudding is sometimes called Plum Pudding. Doctor Johnson, in his seminal dictionary of 1755, defined a plum as a dried fruit, so perhaps he was thinking of prunes as well as raisins, etc. It is such a ragbag, or perhaps "lucky dip" of a dish that it sometimes did include such things.

Every household probably had (and perhaps still has) its own preferred mix. Ingredients varied as to availability, and in times of scarcity substitutes could be found for the more expensive or less easily obtainable ingredients, as for instance, during the Second World War when apples and carrots had to make do for the various dried fruits. Many recipes still contain these as they help to add bulk and substance to the mix.

Christmas puddings have their fans and their detractors. One French visitor in the early 1700's wrote: "*Blessed be he that invented pudding, for it is a manna that hits the palates of all sort of people*". He describes the "*Christmas Pye*" as a "*most learned mixture of Neat's[veal]-Tongues, Chicken, Eggs, Sugar, Raisins, Lemon and Orange Peel, various Kinds of Spicery, etc.*" His opinion was not shared by another Frenchman of a later date, however. In 1824 the French

Almanach des Gourmands characterised it as *"un mélange indigeste et bizarre plutôt qu'une préparation savante et salubre"* – *"an indigestible and bizarre mishmash rather than a sensible and healthy dish"* (my translation).

Making the pudding was one of the most labour-intensive tasks in the Christmas feast. Raisins had to be deseeded, breadcrumbs shredded on a grater (with grated knuckles often an unintended ingredient) orange peel zested, suet shredded – all this was no doubt time-consuming and exhausting.

Yet the excitement generated by the anticipation of the feast – the decoration of the house, the erection of the Christmas tree, the comings and goings, perhaps guests to stay, midnight Mass – all the sense of expectation and difference from ordinary life – carried one along in a sort of haze of anticipatory joy of which the various preparations were simply a part.

The early predecessors of the Christmas pudding contained meat as well as sweet ingredients. Christmas puddings spawned a number of lesser relatives, such as mince pies and Christmas cakes, hence the name "mincemeat" which we still use for the now meatless "mince" pies. A real pudding can always, though, be recognised by the way it is prepared.

Its early predecessors had their ingredients stuffed into the gut or stomach of an animal and either boiled or steamed. From the early 1600's, they began to be wrapped in a cloth while nowadays they are usually enclosed in a pudding bowl.

The Scottish *"cloutie dumplings"*, i.e. puddings boiled in a clout, or cloth, are a continuing element in Scottish cuisine, as is the haggis, another relation which still contains meat as a major ingredient – a throwback to such things as *"a podynge of porpeyse"* dating from the fifteenth century.

As we delve deeper into the pudding itself, its ingredients take us on a journey through cultures and centuries, across the wastes of the Indian and the Atlantic Oceans, from China to America and beyond. They derive from widely-separated peoples such as New Guinea tribesmen, Indian merchants, Mesopotamian agriculturalists, Arab traders, Portuguese and Dutch adventurers, missionaries and plant hunters from Europe.

This extraordinarily rich mid-winter dish, so typically English in its associations, derives from very varied roots. I hope in this small volume to give you a taste of some of this variety, spice and wealth of history and to excite your interest and appreciation, whatever your persuasion regarding its effects on the digestive system.

2oz flour
4oz breadcrumbs
adds SHAPE and
SUBSTANCE

WHEAT

Triticum aestivum L.

TWO OF OUR PUDDING INGREDIENTS, flour and breadcrumbs, are derived from wheat. They form the backbone of the pudding, giving it solidity and structure. They also contribute nutrients in the form of starch, oils and proteins.

The vast wheatfields of North America, the Ukraine, and Australia give little hint of the modest beginnings of this plant somewhere in the region of South-Eastern Turkey and Northern Iraq over 10,000 years ago.

This was where wheat began to be cultivated by ancestral humans. It was the first agricultural revolution and over time it completely changed the way humans lived.

To these early farmers, wheat was so vital to their lives that personified it as a goddess whom the Greeks called Demeter, meaning Corn Mother. As Persephone, she disappeared under the earth for six months every year, then was resurrected and became a life-giving mother at harvest time. In the Eastern Mediterranean, many ancient traditions survive and a variety of special festive dishes in those countries are made using wheat as the main ingredient.

Wheat was so important in Roman society that a special grain allowance was made to each (male) head of household, and the scheme was administered by the emperor himself.

Wheat arrived in the more northerly regions of Europe several hundred years before the advent of the Romans in Britain. Archaeological evidence shows that the crop, once domesticated, spread rapidly from South Eastern Turkey through the countries of Eastern Europe to present-day Germany and further. We know from a Greek traveller called Pyneas that wheat was grown in Britain as early as 330 BC and that huge barns were built to store it, reflecting perhaps the uncertain nature of the British climate. Later on, Roman Britain provided much of the wheat required for the army on the Rhine.

Thousands of mills were recorded in England at the time of the Domesday Book, but mills built by the Romans already existed in Britain. A Roman mill was recently excavated at what is now Ludgate Circus in London, which was operated by the rise and fall of the tides. Tide-mills were highly efficient, combining the naturally recurring energy supply of the sea's surge with immediate proximity to the easiest form of transport of the time – water – so that grain could be delivered and flour distributed direct from the mill.

The storage of flour was always a potential problem, because flour, containing oils and fats, can go rancid if kept for many weeks. This may be one reason why puddings were a good way of preserving it, since they could be (and still can be) kept for many months without going off, and are traditionally prepared up to eighteen months before they are to be eaten.

A Note About Bread

Pitta is a form of flatbread, which was probably the original form which bread took. No-one knows when the properties of yeast were discovered, but it made a very important difference to the taste and texture of bread.

When yeast is added to dough and warmed slightly, carbon dioxide is created. Wheat contains a protein called gluten which 'glues' the bread and prevents the gas from escaping. This allows the dough to rise in the all-important process called proving. When the dough is finally cooked, it results in the loaf familiar to us today.

Bakeries were common in earlier times as many households did not own ovens in which to bake their own bread.

2 tbsp Rum
8oz Muscovado sugar

adds SWEETNESS

SUGAR

Saccharum officinarum L.

SUGAR COMES FROM a giant grass which is native to New Guinea. It was brought north to India where it received the name "*sakkara*" meaning 'gravel' and this name has stuck. The stalks of cane are still used in India as toothbrushes.

From India, Arab traders brought it to Palestine, where large plantations were established. The crusader Knights of St John took it to Cyprus, where a medieval sugar factory was recently excavated. Cyprus sugar was exported to England in the 14th and 15th centuries and was much prized. A visitor to the court of Queen Elizabeth the First noted her black teeth, and wrote that the English had a passion for sugar.

On his second voyage, Columbus brought sugar to the New World, with many other crop plants. Campesinos in Ecuador harvest their own sugar as a cash crop, pressing the cane between two heavy stones worked by a donkey or ox. The resulting syrup is poured into moulds to produce bricks of a greenish colour to take to market. It contains many nutrients and tastes delicious.

Commercially produced sugar is grown in huge plantations and purified until all that remains is a simple substance, white as snow. Such sugar contains little or no nutritive value. It is boiled at very high temperatures and passes through many stages before it is deemed to be ready for sale. Muscovado sugar is less refined, has a strong taste and is dark brown.

Sugar was formerly produced in solid cone-shaped "loaves" and special, sharp sugar tongs were used in order to break pieces off.

RUM is a by-product of sugar which may also be used in the pudding. It can afford an alternative to whisky or brandy, both as an ingredient and for flambéing. A ration of rum, or a watered-down version of it called grog, was formerly given to sailors.

adds
SWEETNESS, BULK,
FLAVOUR and FLAMES

GRAPES

Vitis vinifera L.

10oz currants
8oz sultanas
4oz raisins
Brandy

CURRANTS AND RAISINS are the fruits of the vine, which once grew wild on the shores of the Black Sea. Mankind discovered very early the uses of the clustered fruit, and it was not long before the vine's most widely-used product – wine – was being made.

It is said that the first wine was made in Persia but the earliest records of it come from tomb paintings of Ancient Egypt.

Not all grapes are cultivated for wine. The Muscatel grape, a particularly juicy and aromatic variety, is used also as a table grape, and the sweetest, most succulent raisins, known as sultanas, are usually dried muscatel grapes.

Currants are made from a small black grape, originally grown on the Greek island of Zante. They were traditionally exported from the city of Corinth, or Corauntz, as it was known in medieval times – hence the name.

The Romans cultivated grapes in Britain, and they seem to have been grown here throughout the intervening centuries – but only for wine or to eat fresh – not for drying. At present, 2,500 acres are under grapevines in this country.

Dried grapes were imported into England during the Middle Ages, when cargo ships heading for Dutch ports put in at London, Dover and Plymouth on the way. Raisins and *"Corauntz"* appear frequently in medieval recipes.

In former times, the task of deseeding currants and raisins was a tedious chore in the preparation of a pudding.

Nowadays, many seedless varieties are available, making the cook's task more agreeable. Thompson seedless grapes, a variety developed in California, are now the most widely-used table grapes and raisins.

IN EARLY SPRING delicate almond blossoms cast a bridal veil over the hilly areas of Mediterranean countries – the earliest harbingers of bounty to come. These fruits originate in central Asia, growing wild as far as Turkestan, Afghanistan and Kashmir.

ALMOND TREES prefer a warm temperate climate, and so they spread to the shores of the Mediterranean at an early stage. From there, Phoenician traders took them westward as far as Spain. Today, more than half of commercial almonds are grown in California.

The nut is the kernel of the fruit. It is enclosed in a tough shell, which in turn has a furry outer covering of the palest green. This part of the fruit is the equivalent of the flesh of peaches and apricots, which are closely related to the almond. Tender young almonds, however, can be eaten whole, and in Lebanon for example, these are sold from stalls in the vegetable market and relished as a snack. The characteristic almond flavour is due to the presence of prussic acid, and so, the sweeter the almond, the weaker is its flavour.

In medieval times, milk was not as plentiful as it is now, and also was liable to go off in hot weather. Many early recipes used instead *"milk of amaundes"* which was made from soaking almonds in water. (This is not unlike our present-day way of making coconut milk in the absence of the real thing).

Chopped almonds contribute their indescribable flavour to the pudding. For those who like their crunchy texture, they should only be chopped a little.

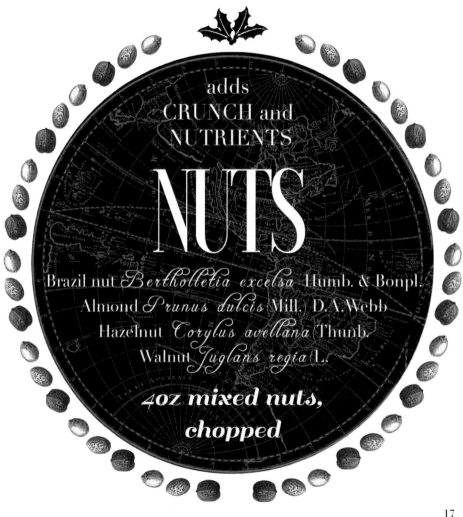

adds
CRUNCH and
NUTRIENTS

NUTS

Brazil nut *Bertholletia excelsa* Humb. & Bonpl.
Almond *Prunus dulcis* (Mill.) D.A.Webb
Hazelnut *Corylus avellana* Thunb.
Walnut *Juglans regia* (L.)

4oz mixed nuts, chopped

HAZELNUTS, cobnuts or filberts are native to Northern Europe, and have been growing in the British Isles ever since the end of the Ice Age. This is evidenced by their appearance in the culture and folk tales of these countries, where they were endowed with magical properties. A hazel rod is the traditional tool used in water divining, thus emphasising the magical properties which it is believed to have.

In Irish mythology, the hazel tree conferred wisdom. It also symbolized the letter C in the Celtic tree alphabet.

Hazel wood has always had many more mundane – and practical – properties. For centuries, hazel coppicing was an important element in the rural economy of these islands. The straight poles were an important building material. Wattle fences kept cattle in and strangers out. House walls were made of hazel rods and clay, in a technique known as wattle and daub. Hazel boughs are flexible, and so were also useful in binding thatch. And the nuts made a nutritious and tasty addition to the winter diet.

Hazel grows all the way across northern Europe, as far as Russia. Its importance was celebrated in The Nutcracker, a ballet often performed at Christmastime.

THE ROMANS INTRODUCED WALNUTS and Spanish Chestnuts to Britain. Walnuts were so highly-prized by the ancients that they called them after Jupiter himself. This is why the botanical name is *Juglans regia*, meaning Jupiter's nut. Spanish, or Sweet, Chestnuts are not usually included in the pudding recipe, but they play an important culinary part since they are used as an accompaniment to turkey.

THE BRAZIL NUT is a fruit of the deep rainforests of the Amazon basin. Many native people in Amazonia are employed in the Brazil nut industry.

The sweet-tasting, oily, extremely nutritious fruits are encased in tough covers like the segments of an orange, and these are tightly packed inside grapefruit-sized spheres made of equally tough woody material. Only the sharp teeth of a small rodent – the agouti – are capable of penetrating the thick cases of the Brazil nut. Like squirrels, these animals then bury some of the fruits, ensuring that new trees will grow. The Brazil nut tree therefore depends on the agouti for its existence.

The tree has an even stranger relationship with a bee and an orchid. There is only one species of bee which visits the Brazil nut flower and so spreads the pollen to other trees. The male bee is only attractive to the female if it has doused itself in the seductive perfume of an orchid, but not just any orchid will do.

Only one particular orchid species possesses the magic formula. Without it, the bees will not mate. And so - without the orchid - no bees. Without the bee, no nut trees. And without the agouti, again there will be no nut trees. This delicately balanced relationship is only one of many throughout the rainforests of the world. It is important for us all that we do not disrupt them.

WHEN THE GERMAN POET GOETHE wrote *"Knows't thou the land where the lemon trees bloom?"* he seems to have felt that the intense colours of citrus fruits glowing among their dark green leaves, symbolised the very spirit of the warm south.

For northerners, the long dark days of winter were enlivened by the festival of Christmas, with its feasting and jollification, and oranges, with their glowing colour, helped to brighten the season. It is traditional to give tangerines in the Christmas stocking as well as putting citrus in the pudding.

Chinese emperors used to receive gifts of oranges, Arab conquerors in Spain grew them in their enclosed gardens, and Portuguese sailors brought sweet oranges to Europe from India.

Columbus brought orange, lemon and citron seedlings to the West Indies, but it was Spanish monks who took them to the West Coast of America. Lemons were brought from India to Europe in Roman times and reintroduced by Arab conquerors in Spain in the 1100's.

adds J

ORANGES

Citrus si

Citrus li

2oz c

grated z

1 lemo

In the seventeenth century, kings and dukes ordered special buildings – orangeries – to be constructed for them, and Nell Gwynn sold them in theatres before becoming intimate with royalty.

Earl Grey tea is flavoured by an orange known as the bergamot, which is also an ingredient in Eau de Cologne. Japanese tea connoisseurs also used an orange to flavour some teas; it was known as a dai-dai.

Squeeze any citrus fruit onto blotting paper, to see the volatile oils from the zest staining the paper. As well as these oils, lemons contain flavonoids, citric acid and citral, as well as dozens of other chemicals which make them valuable in commercial food production.

By adding citrus fruits to the pudding, we are bringing droplets of captured sunshine to the darkest days of winter.

The traditional drink of punch is composed of five ingredients, which includes lemon juice as well as sugar, rum, water and cloves.

CINNAMON HAS A WARM, musky, woody odour, which in the minds of the ancients had distinctly erotic overtones. It is mainly for this indescribable perfume that they valued it.

It is mentioned in the Bible, which tells of the famous visit of the Queen of Sheba to King Solomon. She brought many precious gifts, including various spices. Tradition states that she was bedded by Solomon, although the Bible doesn't say so. Cinnamon is also made much of in the erotic poetry of the Song of Songs.

The Romans used cinnamon as a cosmetic, including it in a type of hair oil.

The funeral pyre of that mythical bird, the Phoenix, was said to consist of frankincense and cinnamon and took place on the island of Socotra, near the Red Sea. The phoenix was a symbol of immortal life and cinnamon was associated with this.

This exotic spice grows in the forests of Sri Lanka, the Serendip of seventeenth century English fantasy. Since 1770 it has been widely cultivated in Java, Indonesia, East Africa and the West Indies but the best quality cinnamon still comes from Sri Lanka. The spice is obtained from the layer of inner bark – the cambium – of the cinnamon tree.

After three years, the young trees are coppiced, which results in the growth of long straight branches. A further three years on, they are harvested for the first time.

The inner bark contains the aromatic substances which give the spice its flavour. This is largely due to a volatile oil called cinnamic aldehyde, but many more compounds are involved in the creation of cinnamon's delicate flavour. This taste is considered to be altogether more desirable than a substance which is often used as a substitute for cinnamon, namely cassia.

Research has shown that cinnamon has potential in the treatment of diabetes, as it mimics insulin and helps to regulate sugar levels.

1/2 teaspoon
ground cinnamon

CINNAMON

Cinnamomum zeylanicum Breyne

adds WARM FRAGRANCE

1/2 teaspoon
ground cloves

adds CARNATION FRAGRANCE
and FIERY TASTE

CLOVES

Syzygium aromaticum
[L.] Merr. et Perry

"Nose, nose, nose, nose!
And who gave thee that jolly red nose?
Sinament and Ginger, Nutmegs and Cloves,
And that gave me my jolly red nose."
Beaumont and Fletcher's "The Knight of the Burning Pestle"

CLOVES, LIKE NUTMEGS, originate in the Moluccas, islands south-west of Java. The little nail-like black objects release a perfume reminiscent of summer's carnations. This is not surprising, as they are themselves flowerbuds, picked before the flowers open out fully.

The name clove is a corruption of the French word for a nail, *"clou"*, on account of their shape.

Despite the fragrant smell of the clove, if you bite into one the sensation is not only extremely bitter, but it also has a powerful anaesthetic effect. This is why it was often recommended for toothache, and it works – at least until the numbing effect wears off. In ancient China, officials going to meet the emperor were advised to chew cloves beforehand in order to avoid offending him with bad breath.

Recent research has shown that cloves may be useful in cleaning up sites contaminated by asbestos. Tiny fragments of asbestos float in the air and enter the lungs of people working with it, causing the fatal ailment asbestosis. One of cloves' constituent oils forms a polymer with these particles and thus anchors them and prevents them from floating in the air.

THE GINGER FAMILY, unequalled for the range and power of its flavours, includes turmeric and cardamom as well as others such as grains of paradise, zedoary and galangal, which were familiar in the Middle Ages.

Ginger flowers are fragrant and beautiful, but it is the fleshy rhizome which has been prized from ancient times as a spice and as a medicine. Ginger is a plant of the hot tropics.

It is an essential ingredient in Chinese cooking, and its medicinal qualities have long been valued by mankind. It is often used against travel sickness. It helps digestion, and besides contains all sorts of "good" antioxidants, thus helping to ward off cancer.

Prehistoric sailors of the Eastern Pacific used to take live ginger, rooted in pots, with them on their voyages. This not only shows that they had a high appreciation of culinary variety, but they may also have used the plant as a preventative against scurvy.

Recipes in former times often called for powdered ginger. Nowadays the growth of air transport means that fresh ginger root is a commonplace of our kitchen cupboards.

1 level teaspoon
grated ginger

GINGER

Zingiber officinale Roscoe

adds HEAT & SPICE

THE CARIBBEAN ISLAND OF GRENADA, a green speck rising from an azure sea, and bathed in mild ocean breezes, provides the perfect environment for the nutmeg tree, and Grenada supplies much of the world's demand for this delectable spice.

Grenada, however, was not its first home. Nutmeg was one of the rarest of the spices in the medieval cupboard, as it originated in a single group of islands - the Bandas. These are hundreds of miles from the main island group, lying somewhere between Java and Australia, and virtually inaccessible even today.

The fruit is the seed of the nutmeg tree, and mace, another spice, is wrapped around the nut like scarlet lace. Local people make jam from the pulp of the fruit.

Dutch soldiers, arriving in the seventeenth century, cut down and burned the wild trees in an attempt to retain the monopoly of the spice trade. This they were eventually unable to do as pigeons, flying over, are said to have carried the seeds to other islands.

Pigeons or no pigeons, a Frenchman with the very apt name of *Pierre Poivre* (Peter Pepper), managed to smuggle some seed out, and planted them in Reunion, Madagascar and Mauritius in the 1770's thus breaking the monopoly of the Dutch.

Rumour has it that a British trader who had lived the South East Asia and moved to Grenada in the Eighteenth century, missed the nutmeg in his rum punch so much that he arranged to have some nutmeg trees brought there.

Grenadan rum punches are in themselves worth a visit to the island.

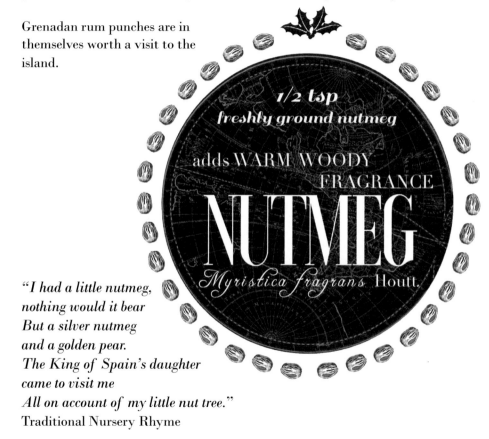

1/2 tsp
freshly ground nutmeg

adds WARM WOODY
FRAGRANCE

NUTMEG

Myristica fragrans Houtt.

"I had a little nutmeg,
nothing would it bear
But a silver nutmeg
and a golden pear.
The King of Spain's daughter
came to visit me
All on account of my little nut tree."
Traditional Nursery Rhyme

1 sprig
fresh holly

adds DECORATION

HOLLY

Ilex aquifolium L.

"*Of all the trees that are in the wood, the holly bears the crown.*"

Old English Christmas Carol '*The Holly and the Ivy*'

WHEN THE FLAMING PUDDING is borne to the table, fragrant and steaming, the crowning touch is the sprig of holly, with its bright red berries and dark green leaves.

Because holly is one of our native trees, it has many mythological associations. Holly was always an important player in the midwinter festival.

It was revered in pagan times as a plant which had magical properties. Symbolising fertility, this was one of the few plants - apart from the rather sinister yew - which had red fruit and remained green in the depths of winter.

It was considered to be unlucky to cut down a holly tree, although the upper, thornless leaves, were gathered as cattle fodder in severe winters, when other sources of animal feed were in short supply.

Holly wood is hard and white, and so has been used as a substitute for ivory, in piano keys and chess pieces. Paradoxically, because it easily takes a dye, it can also be made to imitate ebony.

The wood was traditionally used to make horsewhips, in part because of its supposed magical ability to control horses.

It was believed that holly could protect a household from evil spirits, and so it was brought into the house, along with another evergreen plant, ivy, to celebrate the turn of the year, and the hoped-for return of the sun. With its bright colours it still has the power to cheer us up in those dark days.

A Recipe for *Christmas* PUDDING

This recipe makes one large pudding in a two-pint bowl, and should feed 8 -10 people.

INGREDIENTS

2 oz (50 gr) self-raising flour
4 oz wholemeal bread crumbs
1/2 teaspoon ground cloves
1/2 teaspoon freshly grated nutmeg
1/2 teaspoon ground cinnamon
1 level teaspoon of grated ginger
8 oz (225gr) muscovado sugar
4 oz (110 gr) shredded suet

4 oz (110 gr)raisins
8 oz(110gr sultanas
10 oz (275 gr) currants
2oz (25 gr) mixed candied peel, finely chopped
4 oz mixed nuts, chopped
1 small cooking apple, peeled, cored and finely chopped
Grated zest and juice of an orange
Grated zest and juice of a lemon
5 fluid ounces stout
2 tablespoons rum or brandy
2 large eggs

Start preparing the ingredients the day before you intend to cook your pudding. Put the flour, breadcrumbs, spices, sugar and suet in your biggest mixing bowl, followed by the dried fruits, nuts and peels. Then add the apple, and the grated orange and lemon zest and juice. Ticking off each item as you go is helpful to keep track.

Next measure out the rum or brandy, stout and eggs and beat them thoroughly together. Pour this over all the other ingredients and begin to mix very thoroughly, adding more stout if it is too stiff. It should drop quite easily off the spoon. This is the stage when everyone gets a chance to stir and make a wish, if they feel inclined. Leave it overnight covered with a towel. Carefully spoon the mixture into a suitable bowl for steaming.

If you like, tie a piece of string across the top to make a handle. Boil some water in a deep pan, and when it is bubbling nicely place a steamer over the pan and put the pudding basin in it. You can cover the pudding with the lid of the pan to keep the steam in and the temperature up.

Now comes the boring bit. The pudding has to boil/steam for eight hours. During this time, the water will probably boil off, maybe more than once. This means that someone (probably the cook) has to keep an eye on it during that time.

The water also has to be topped up from time to time. This fresh water must be boiling as you pour it on, otherwise the pudding will taste of congealed suet (these are my own personal observations).

When the pudding is steamed let it get quite cold, then remove the papers and foil and replace them with some fresh ones, again making a string handle for easier manoeuvring. Keep it in a cool place away from the light.

To reheat, stand in boiling water to half the height of the basin and cook for 2½ hours. Turn out the pudding carefully on a fireproof plate. If you have it, place your holly sprig on top at this stage.

Warm two tablespoons of rum, brandy, or whisky in a saucepan. When warm, light it in the saucepan, and carefully pour the flaming liquid over the pudding.

Serve with rum butter, hard sauce, or sherry sauce.

Mrs Beeton's Recipe, 1861

Christmas Plum Pudding (Very Good)

1½lb Raisins
12oz Fresh Breadcrumbs
12oz Suet
8oz Currants
8oz Mixed Peel
8 Eggs
1 glass Brandy

MODE

Stone and cut the raisins in halves, but do not chop them; wash, pick, and dry the currants, and mince the suet finely; cut the candied peel into thin slices, and grate down the bread into fine crumbs.

When all these dry ingredients are prepared, mix them well together; then moisten the mixture with the eggs, which should be well beaten, and the brandy; stir well, that everything may be very thoroughly blended, and press the pudding into a buttered mould; tie it down tightly with a floured cloth, and boil for 5 or 6 hours.

It may be boiled in a cloth without a mould, and will require the same time allowed for cooking. As Christmas puddings are usually made a few days before they are required for table, when the pudding is taken out of the pot, hang it up immediately, and put a plate or saucer underneath to catch the water that may drain from it. The day it is to be eaten, plunge it into boiling water, and keep it boiling for at least 2 hours; then turn it out of the mould, and serve with brandy-sauce. On Christmas day a sprig of holly is usually placed in the middle of the pudding, and about a wineglassful of brandy poured round it, which, at the moment of serving, is lighted, and the pudding thus brought to table encircled in flame.

TIME
5 or 6 hours the first time of boiling; 2 hours the day it is to be served. Sufficient for a quart mould for 7 or 8 persons. Seasonable on the 25th of December and on various festive occasions until March.

Note the absence of flour, spices and sugar in this recipe, hence the very generous proportions of dried fruit.

Scripture Pudding
A Riddle for a Recipe

The following recipe is from Amish sources in the USA.

4 ½ cups	Kings IV 22
1 ½ cup	Judges V 25
2 cups	Jeremiah VI 30
1 cups	I Samuel XXX 12
2 cups	Nahum III 12
1 cup	Numbers XVII 8
2 teaspoons	I Samuel XIV 25
Six	Jeremiah XVII 2
1 ½ cups	Judges IV 19
2 teaspoons	Amos IV 5
A pinch of	Leviticus II 13

Season to taste with II Chronicles IX 9

Directions: Proverbs XXIII 14

Solution

"Behold, there was a cake baken"
I Kings: 9-16

Kings IV 22: *Fine flour*
Judges V 25: *Butter*
Jeremiah VI 30: *Sugar*
I Samuel XXX 12: *Raisins*
Nahum III 12: *Ripe figs*
Numbers XVII 8: *Almonds*
I Samuel XIV 25: *Honey*
Jeremiah XVII 2: *Eggs*
Judges IV 19: *Milk*
Amos IV 5: *Leaven*
Leviticus II 13: *Salt*
II Chronicles IX 9: *Spice*

Proverbs XXIII 14: *Beat*

Some Sources & further reading

Davidson, Alan: The Oxford Companion to Food. *OUP 1999*

Drummond, Jack and Anne Wilbraham: The Englishman's Food. *Cape, 1957*

David, Elizabeth: English Bread and Yeast Cookery. *Penguin, 2001*

O'Connell, Sanjida: Sugar. *Virgin Books, 2004*

Spiegel-Roy and E Goldschmidt: Biology of Citrus. *CUP, 1996*

Thirsk, Joan: Food in Early Modern England. *Hambledon Continuum, 2008*

Turner, Jack: Spice, the History of a Temptation. *Harper Collins, 2007*